Title: Letters I'll Never Send: A Ritual for Closure and Release. ™

Copyright © 2025 Erin Hubbard. All rights reserved.
Published by Shelf Nine Publishing.

No part of this publication may be reproduced, distributed, or transmitted in any form or by any means, including photocopying, recording, or other electronic or mechanical methods, without the prior written permission of the publisher, except in the case of brief quotations embodied in reviews and certain other noncommercial uses permitted by copyright law.

For permission requests, write to the publisher at:
info@shelfninepublishing.com
First Edition
Hardback ISBN: 978-1-967749-04-1
Printed in the United States of America.

This Book Belongs To:

_____

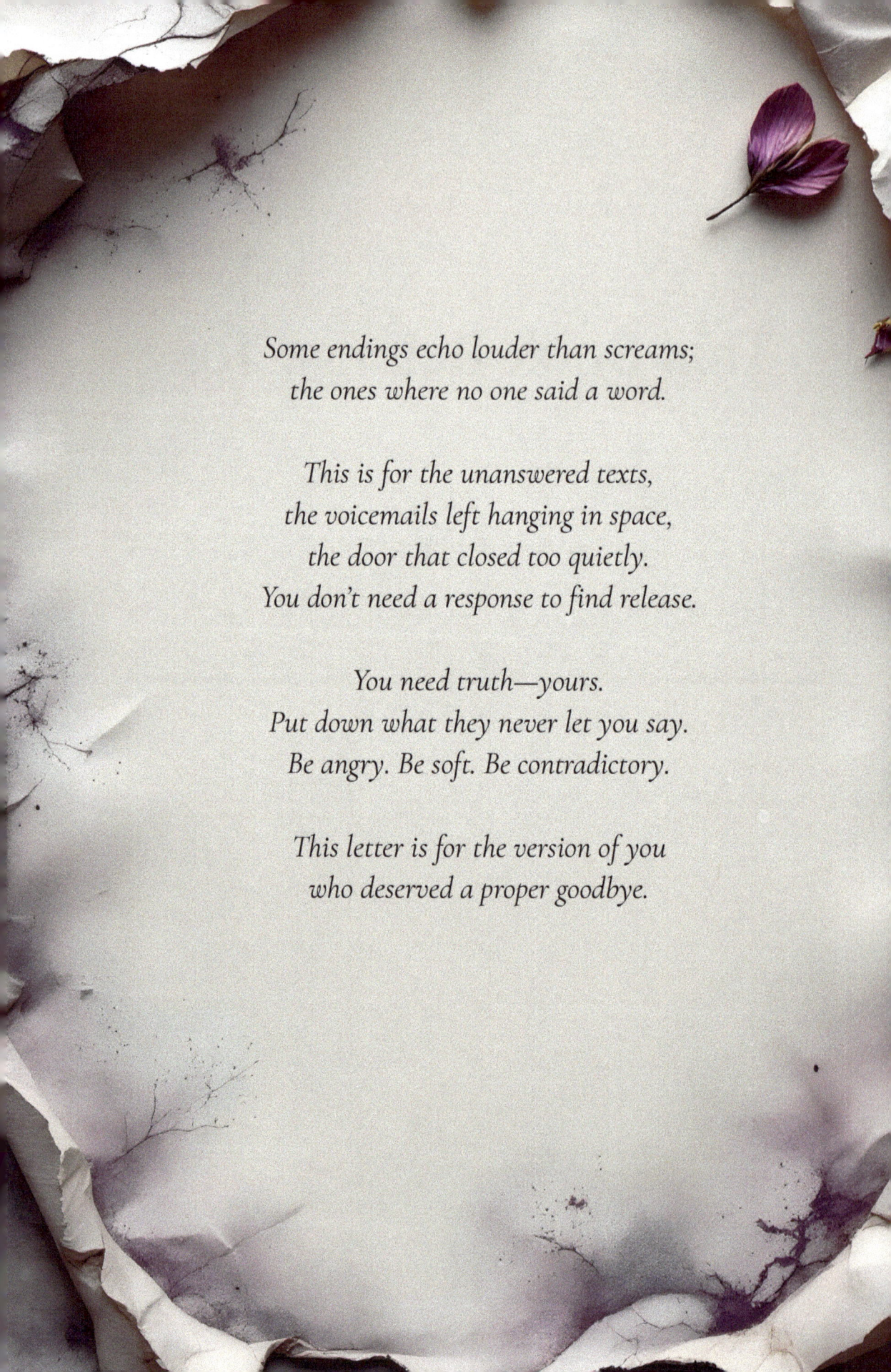

Some endings echo louder than screams;
the ones where no one said a word.

This is for the unanswered texts,
the voicemails left hanging in space,
the door that closed too quietly.
You don't need a response to find release.

You need truth—yours.
Put down what they never let you say.
Be angry. Be soft. Be contradictory.

This letter is for the version of you
who deserved a proper goodbye.

A LETTER TO THE ONE WHO DIDN'T SAY GOODBYE

When you're done, leave it in the book or tear it out and burn it safely.

Let it leave your hands like it once left your heart.

There was a version of you who dreamed freely,
who trusted someone who didn't deserve it,
who laughed without needing to be careful.

You left them behind to survive;
maybe out of necessity, maybe out of fear.
And maybe you never stopped waiting for you to come back.

Write to the you who never got closure.

The one who didn't get to choose what happened.

Let it be messy, and kind, and raw.

To the Version of Me I Abandoned

You called it love when it was manipulation.
When it was control. When it was neglectful silence.
When things only moved forward if I broke myself
down into smaller pieces.

I told myself you meant well.
I made excuses with my entire being.
I thought if I could just fix me, you'd stop hurting me.

Write to the version of yourself that believed them.
Write to the liar, too. If you want.

You don't owe them kindness. You owe you truth.
Say it all, without being gentle it this time.

To the One Who Lied and Called It Love

They arrive when the world has gone quiet.
In the memories you beg the sky to forget.

A name you no longer say out loud,
but your buried thoughts still scream.
It's the ache that surfaces
when sleep avoids
you.

A flicker of something unfinished,
still walking the halls of your mind.

Maybe they were never yours.
Maybe they still are.
Maybe you're tired of wondering.

This isn't about going back.

Write without edits.

Let the stillness break wide open.

You were never too much.
You were just surrounded by someone who didn't know what to do with real.

They called it too sensitive. Needy. Dramatic.
But it wasn't you; it was them, running from the depth they couldn't comprehend.

You didn't need saving.
You needed someone who saw you and didn't look away.

Speak to the version of you who didn't know what love was supposed to feel like.

The one who smiled to survive. Who waited for the bare minimum and called it connection.

Say what no one ever did.

You're not waiting anymore.

To My Younger Self Who Deserved More

There are silences that scream louder than words.
This one was a sentence that never ended.

A door that stayed shut, even when you knocked with your whole heart…. your entire existence.

This isn't about what they should've said.
It's about what you deserved to hear.

The acknowledgment. The ownership. The undoing of pain.

Give yourself the words you waited for.
Let them take up space.
Then reclaim them; not as closure, but as clarity.

To the Apology I Never Received

I didn't always live inside this body.
Sometimes I fled it. Sometimes I numbed it.
Sometimes I wished I could unzip it and leave it behind.

This is for the shoulders that carried more than they should have.
The stomach that clenched to keep the peace.

The need you silenced when it asked to be seen.
The weight you carried long after it should've been put down.

Accept the parts of yourself you once tried to escape.
Not to blame them, just to return to them.
You don't have to love them yet. Just stop running.

To the Body I Didn't Feel Safe In

It didn't start with a fight.

It started with shorter replies. Delayed responses.
Less laughter. Less "I made this thing and thought of you."
And then it wasn't "us" anymore.
It was just time passing by.

A quiet that nobody questioned. A drifting nobody stopped.

This letter isn't to reignite.
It's to say what was never said before it was too late.

Put words to the version of you who kept reaching until
your hand stayed in the air, alone.

Write to the space that filled up between you.

Not to fix it. But to finally hear yourself in the quiet.

To the Space You Let Grow Between Us

You weren't chosen. You were auditioning.

Hoping if you gave more, shrank more, smiled more,
they would finally see you as enough.

This letter isn't about blame.
It's about the exhaustion that comes from never being picked
unless you disappear first.

Write to the one who stayed, even after the affection turned
cold.

And to the effort that went unrewarded and to the version of
you that believed love had to be earned at all.

Let this be the last time you beg for crumbs.

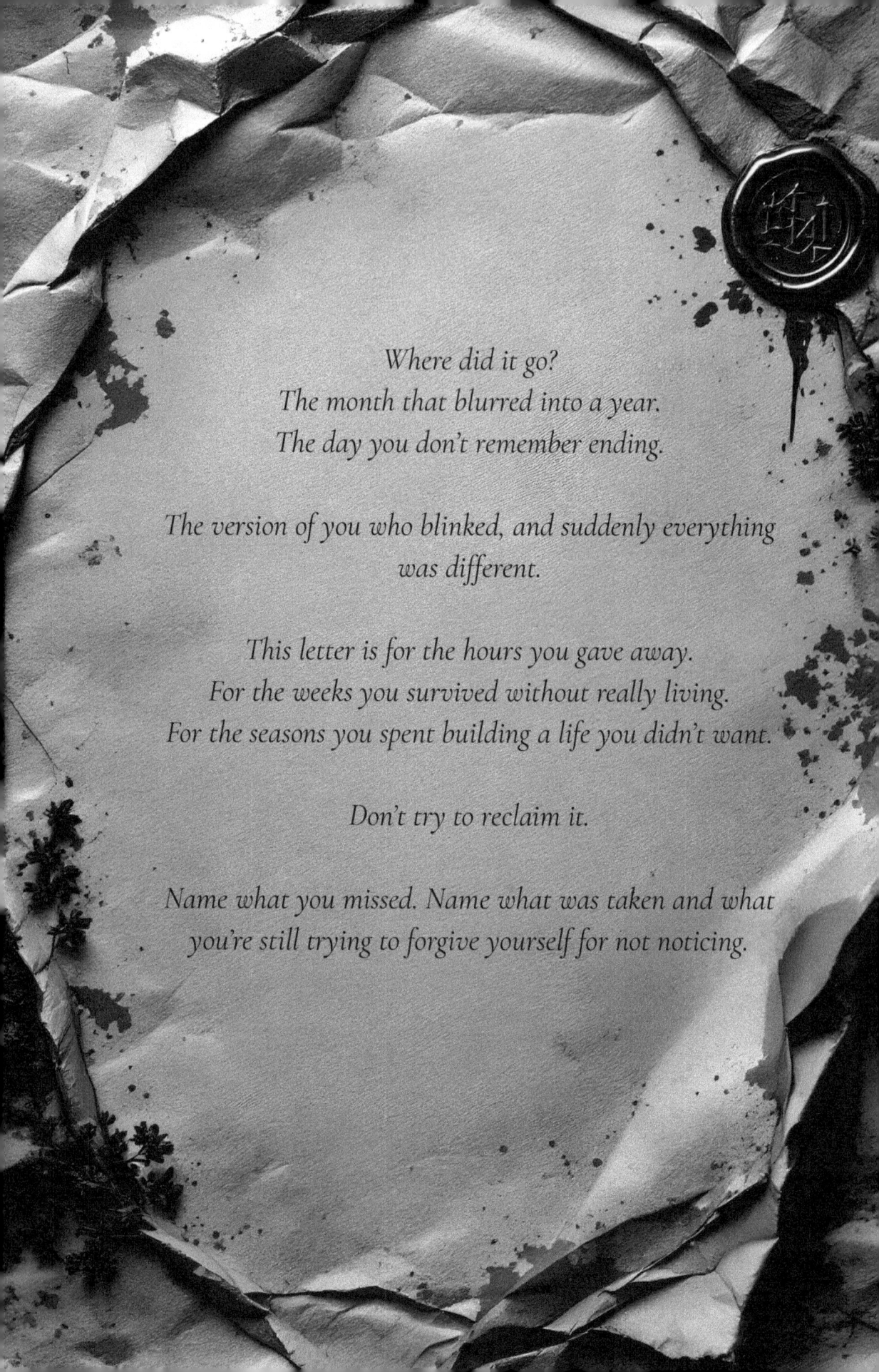

Where did it go?
The month that blurred into a year.
The day you don't remember ending.

The version of you who blinked, and suddenly everything was different.

This letter is for the hours you gave away.
For the weeks you survived without really living.
For the seasons you spent building a life you didn't want.

Don't try to reclaim it.

Name what you missed. Name what was taken and what you're still trying to forgive yourself for not noticing.

To the Time I Lost

*It wasn't supposed to end like that.
Maybe it wasn't supposed to end at all.
Maybe it wasn't even suppose to begin.*

But there it was, the final moment. Uninvited. Unexplained.

*You tried to fix it.
You held the threads,
as if that could keep it all from unraveling.
But you can't stitch something closed when the fabric keeps vanishing.*

This is where you say what you couldn't say then.

Not to erase it, just to expose it.

So it doesn't keep whispering back every time something else ends.

To the Ending I Didn't Want

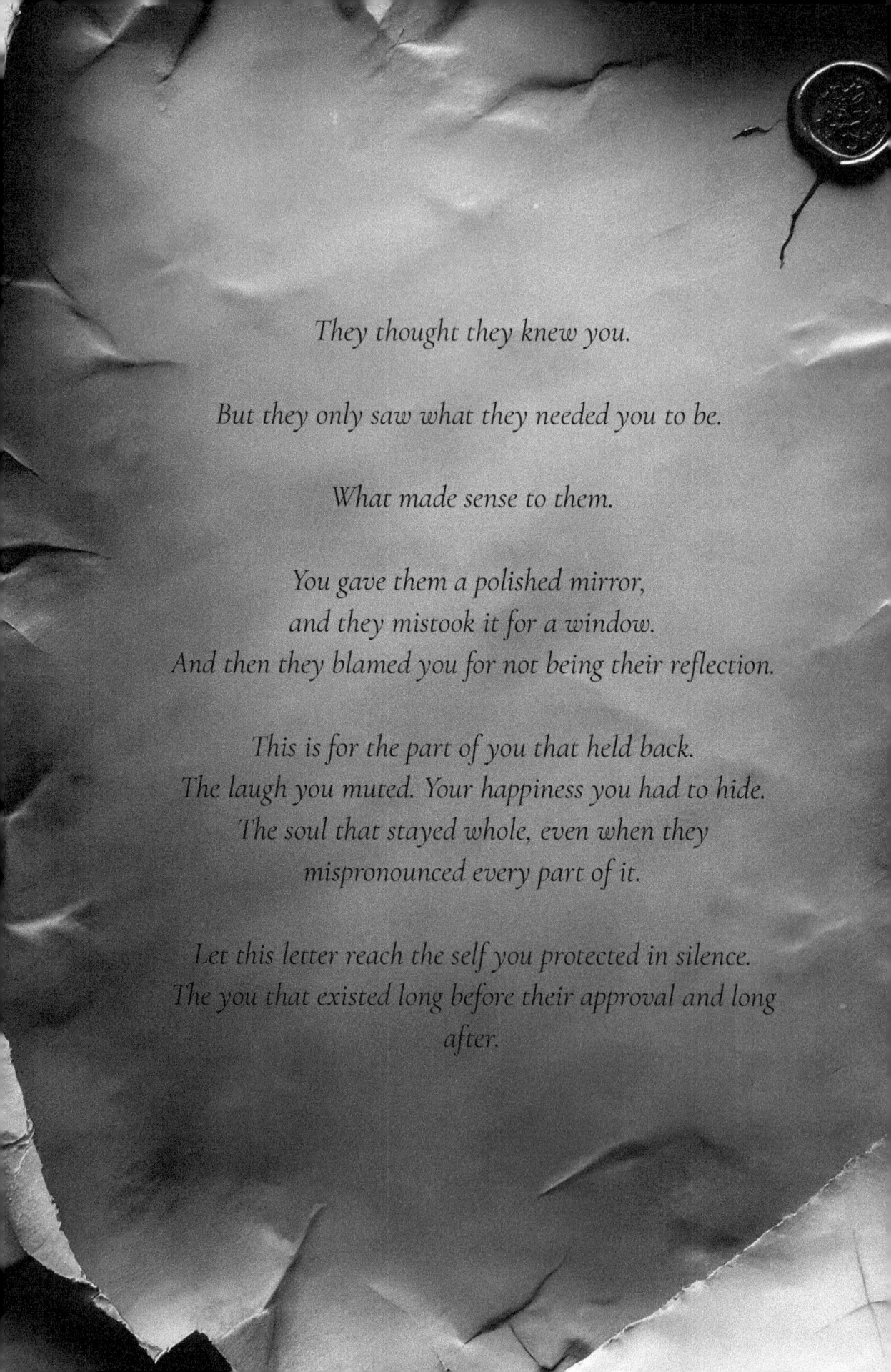

They thought they knew you.

But they only saw what they needed you to be.

What made sense to them.

You gave them a polished mirror,
and they mistook it for a window.
And then they blamed you for not being their reflection.

This is for the part of you that held back.
The laugh you muted. Your happiness you had to hide.
The soul that stayed whole, even when they
mispronounced every part of it.

Let this letter reach the self you protected in silence.
The you that existed long before their approval and long
after.

To the Version of Me They Never Really Knew

You knew.

Maybe not at first, but eventually you did.
And still, you stayed.
You reasoned.
You made yourself smaller.
You called it patience.
You called it hope.
But hope is a loyal beast, even to those who don't feed it.

This is the letter to the moment you ignored.
The red flag you repainted white.
The part of you that whispered "this isn't it" and was silenced.

Write to the one who lingered too long in someone else's story.
You don't owe them a goodbye.
But maybe you owe that version of yourself one.

To the One I Should Have Let Go Sooner

You stood at the threshold, didn't you?
One foot in the past, one hand on the door to the future.

Waiting for them to apologize.
Waiting for yourself to feel ready.
Waiting for life to stop hurting long enough to begin.

This is for the part of you that built a home out of hesitation.
Who paused joy, postponed healing, and stood still for false promises.

Speak to the part of you who waited.
For love. For permission. For the storm to end.
Let them know it's safe to leave the doorway now.

To the Part of Me That Always Waited

You stopped dreaming because it hurt too much to wish.

You called it realism.
You called it survival.
But really, it was a quiet self-collapse.

You just didn't think you'd make it.
This is for the version of you that always prepared for endings, not beginnings.

Who learned to hide at the idea of joy.
Who mistook "peace" for waiting on the next storm.

Acknowledge here the life you never let yourself imagine.
The one you didn't think you deserved.

Let it know you're coming, even if you're still afraid.

To the Future I Was Afraid to Imagine

The lie gave you comfort. The truth gave you clarity.
But clarity isn't always clean. Sometimes it guts you.
Sometimes it rips through the fantasy and leaves you holding your own bones.

This is the letter you write after the illusion breaks.
Not to mourn the lie, but to honor what it cost to see the truth.

To say, "I saw it. I stayed anyway. And now I know better."

Write to the moment the truth arrived,
and you finally let it in.

To the Truth That Hurt More Than the Lie

There were days you couldn't even look at yourself.
You said you were tired.
You said you were fine.
You said nothing.

But your reflection knew the truth.
It always did.

This is for the self you avoided.
The skin you couldn't live in.
The version of you who stood there,
silent, waiting for you to come home.

Write to the face you once hid from.
Let it be seen now. Let it be loved—flaws, scars, and all.

To the Mirror I Couldn't Look Into

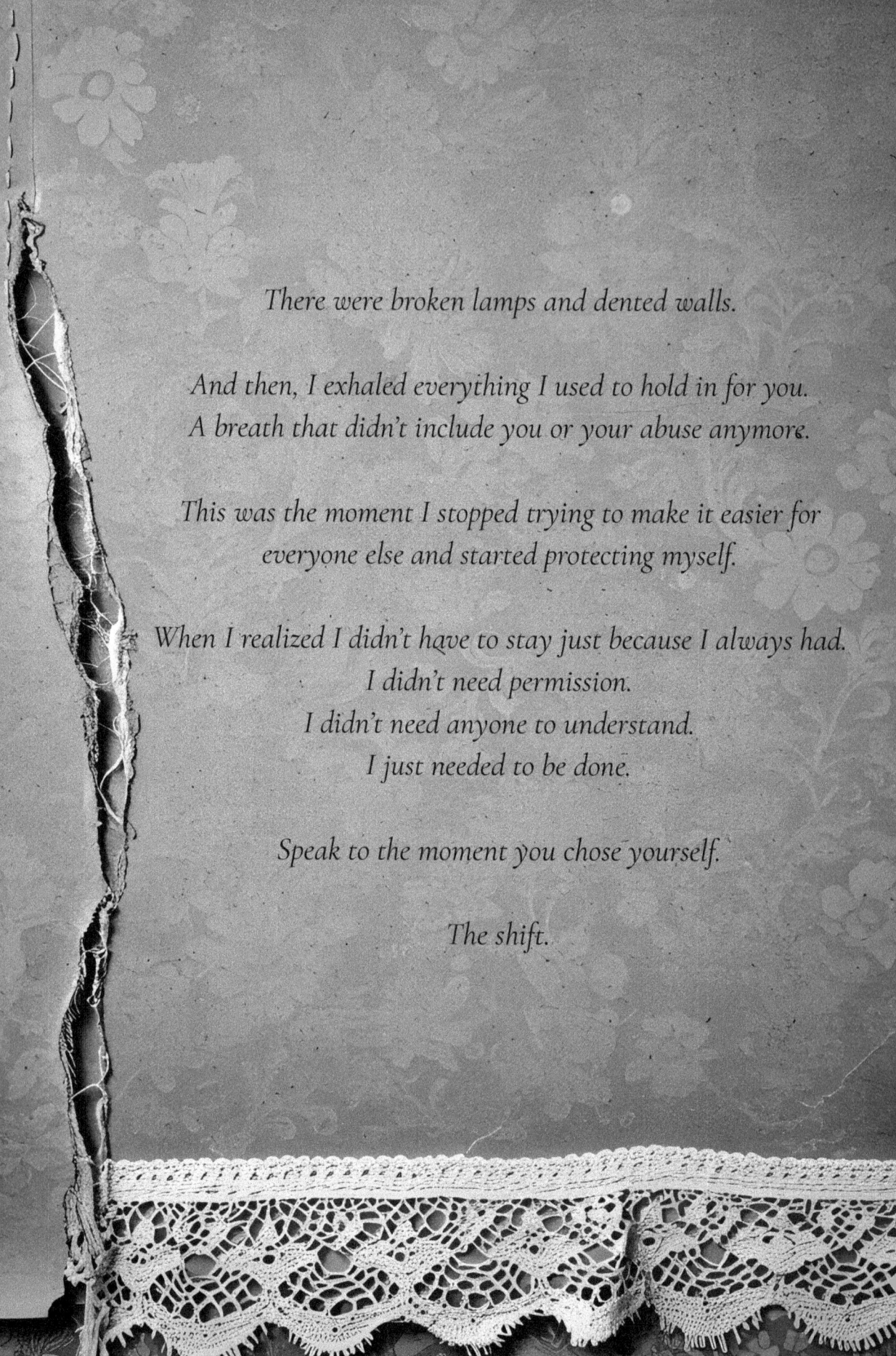

There were broken lamps and dented walls.

And then, I exhaled everything I used to hold in for you.
A breath that didn't include you or your abuse anymore.

This was the moment I stopped trying to make it easier for
everyone else and started protecting myself.

When I realized I didn't have to stay just because I always had.
I didn't need permission.
I didn't need anyone to understand.
I just needed to be done.

Speak to the moment you chose yourself.

The shift.

<u>To the Moment I Finally Let It Burn</u>

You don't have to rewrite the past.

You don't have to explain it to anyone.

You lived it.
You carried it.
You survived it.

And now, you get to choose
what never gets to follow you home again.

Erin Hubbard is a multi-genre author and the founder of Shelf Nine Publishing, a publishing company dedicated to bold, original storytelling. Her work ranges from humorous children's books to emotionally immersive nonfiction that explores silence, survival, and self-reclamation. With a background in psychology, she has a particular interest in the inner complexities of the human experience and a strong desire to help others and nurture the mind through writing.

Letters I'll Never Send invites readers to write what was never allowed to be spoken. It is not just a guide, it is a space for release.

She lives and creates in Florida, always surrounded by notebooks, organic coffee, and one too many open tabs.

www.ingramcontent.com/pod-product-compliance
Lightning Source LLC
Chambersburg PA
CBHW061358010526
44107CB00012B/972